DOWN THE DRAIN

THE SCIENCE OF CLEANING WATER

BY
LESLEY NEWSON

ILLUSTRATED BY
MIKE GORDON

SIMON & SCHUSTER

LONDON • SYDNEY • NEW YORK • TOKYO • SINGAPORE • TORONTO

First published in Great Britain in 1990
by Simon & Schuster Young Books

Simon & Schuster Young Books
Simon & Schuster International Group
Wolsey House, Wolsey Road
Hemel Hempstead HP2 4SS

British Library Cataloguing in Publication Data
Newson, Lesley
  Down the drain.
  1. Water. Purification
  I. Title
  628.162

  ISBN 0–7500–0274–3

Printed in Great Britain by BPCC Wheatons Ltd, Exeter

Contents

A Close Look at
Dirty Water

Your family pulls the plug on over 1,000 litres of dirty water every day. Have you ever thought what that water is taking with it as it gurgles and flushes its way down the drain?

The water that drains away from your bath or shower contains dirt, sweat and grease from your skin and hair. It washes away hairs that have fallen out and flakes of dead skin. And it contains the chemicals like soap, shampoo and bubble bath that you used to help clean yourself.

When you flush the toilet you are washing away urine, faeces and toilet paper. Urine contains most of the waste chemicals that your body has to get rid of in order to keep you healthy. Faeces also contain some waste chemicals, but they are mostly made up of bits of food that you can't digest and billions of bacteria.

House cleaning, washing up and doing the laundry produce lots more dirty water full of grease, dust, bits of food and the chemicals we use for cleaning and disinfecting.

In some kitchens there is a grinder underneath the sink so that kitchen waste like potato peelings and uneaten food can be chopped up small enough to go down the drain. Hair, cigarette ends, plastic and even clothing can all be seen floating along in the water that flows out of our drains and into the sewers.

Have you ever wondered what happens to all this water and the dirt it contains? Where does it go? Does it cause any harm?

A Close Look at Clean Water

Your family turns the tap on over 1,000 litres of clean water every day. Have you ever wondered how it got there and how it is possible for such huge amounts of water to be delivered to every home?

The water that comes out of your taps isn't new water freshly made for you. It was made about 4,000 million years ago and it has been used and dirtied many times since then because it flows round in a continuous cycle. The water in your tap might well have been flushing down someone else's drain a few weeks ago. And your bath water might soon be someone else's cup of tea.

If you think too hard about where your water might have been, it could put you off drinking it. But it doesn't matter if your water comes in orange juice, a soft drink or milk, it is always very old and very used water. And, just like every other living creature on Earth, you need this water to stay alive.

ALL THE WATER IN THIS ESTABLISHMENT HAS BEEN PASSED BY THE MANAGEMENT!

Living creatures have survived on Earth for thousands of millions of years using and reusing the same water because the Earth's water supply is continuously being cleaned. It happens quite naturally. Clean water comes out of our taps because scientists and engineers have learned to work in partnership with Nature and have built water systems to clean water and deliver it to our homes.

But there are problems. Many of our water systems don't work as well as they should.

Human beings use (and dirty) more water than any other animal and sometimes the dirty water is being allowed to pollute rivers, lakes and oceans. In some areas, people are unhappy about the way their water tastes, smells or looks, or suspect that their tap water might be unhealthy to drink.

And the people who are worrying about these problems are the lucky ones. Most people in the world do not have clean water on tap. In some countries it is very common for people to fall ill and even die from drinking water that is contaminated with harmful bacteria.

We will only be able to solve today's water problems by working more closely with Nature and taking care not to damage the Earth's natural water cleaning systems.

The Solar Powered Water Purifier

There is an awful lot of water on Earth. Scientists have calculated that it amounts to about 1,400,000,000,000,000,000,000 litres. But only a tiny proportion of this water is fit for us to drink. About 97 per cent of it, for example, is in the salty oceans. But the water on Earth is always on the move and water that is undrinkable one day can be perfectly clean the next.

Anyone who has hung clothes out to dry knows that water evaporates and becomes part of the air. On a reasonably dry day, liquid water turns into a gas (or vapour) and rises through the atmosphere. This is true wherever water is – in your clothes, an ocean, lake, river, puddle or on the surface of your skin. All over the Earth, about 100,000,000,000,000 litres of water rise into the atmosphere every day.

This is the first of the Earth's water cleaning systems and it can provide the cleanest water of all. It works because only the water evaporates. Salt, soil, soap, grease, seaweed and everything else that was in the water when it was a liquid, is left behind.

The water vapour in the air doesn't just rise, it moves about with the wind, spreading all over the Earth. In time, it gets colder and turns back into liquid water. This is called 'condensing'. If the water vapour gets very cold, it turns into ice crystals. No matter how dirty the water was before it evaporated, it is always pure at the moment it turns back into liquid water.

The water can continue to travel through the air as clouds of tiny water droplets or ice crystals for a while, but when conditions are right, they join together and eventually become heavy enough to fall out of the clouds and back down to the Earth as rain, snow, or hail.

You can evaporate and condense some water yourself to see how well it cleans. Collect some of your dirty washing up or bath water in a saucepan.

You will also need:
– a frying pan large enough to more than cover the top of the saucepan but light enough for you to handle
– a cup to collect the clean water
– a pair of oven gloves
– permission to use the stove and an adult standing by.

evaporate. Put on the oven gloves and hold the frying pan upside down about 10 centimetres above the saucepan. After half a minute or so, take the frying pan away from the saucepan and gently turn it over. Has a fine covering of water droplets begun to collect on the surface of the frying pan?

Hold the frying pan upside down over the saucepan again. (Be sure not to put your face, hands or

Heat the dirty water on the hotplate. As the water gets warmer, more and more of it will start to

arms over the saucepan. The rising water vapour will get hot enough to give you a serious scald.) As the water gets warmer, more vapour will rise and then condense to liquid again as it reaches the frying pan. Eventually some of the water will form into drops and start to fall down again just like the raindrops fall out of the clouds. If you tilt the frying pan, most of the water will run downward and dribble off one side. Collect the drops in a cup.

Once you have collected a few spoonfuls of water in the cup, turn off the heat and carefully put down the frying pan. (It will be quite hot.) Other substances could also have evaporated from the saucepan and risen the short distance up to the frying pan. Even so, the water collected on your frying pan will be a lot cleaner than the original dirty water.

Imagine how high our gas or electricity bills would be if we had to clean all our water by evaporating and condensing it. It's lucky for us and all other living things that the Earth has a natural water purification system. The energy to make water evaporate is provided free by the Sun and the condensation happens automatically in the cool air far above our heads.

WATER
PURIFICATION
PLANT
TOURS
5p.

SUN

WATER

The Living Cleaners

The first thing to forget if you are trying to understand the science of cleaning water is the idea that clean water and pure water are the same. The safest, clearest and nicest-tasting water on Earth is far from pure. And pure water isn't really very useful. Fish can't live in it and nor can any other living thing. In fact, it is water's ability to collect impurities that makes it essential to life on Earth. And living things are essential for cleaning water.

The tiny droplets of water that condense from cooling water vapour may be perfectly pure when they form, but they begin to pick up impurities when they are still in the clouds. The oxygen, nitrogen and carbon dioxide gases that make up the air mix with water and so do particles of dust and chemicals that are in the air. And once the water falls to the ground as rain, it really begins to collect impurities.

If the rainwater falls on land, it gradually travels toward the sea, picking up impurities as it goes. Some of it flows on the surface of the ground joining streams and rivers until it reaches the sea. The rest seeps into the earth. It may cling to soil and be taken up by the roots of plants or it may continue to sink and become part of the 'groundwater'. (More about this in Chapter 6.)

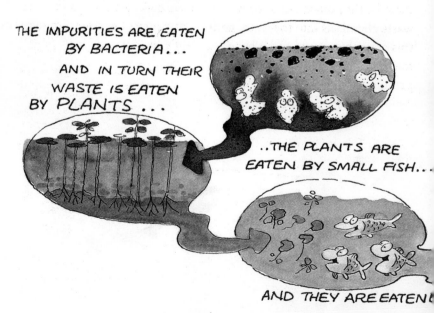

THE IMPURITIES ARE EATEN BY BACTERIA... AND IN TURN THEIR WASTE IS EATEN BY PLANTS ...

..THE PLANTS ARE EATEN BY SMALL FISH...

AND THEY ARE EATEN

As the water travels to the sea, it picks up minerals from the rocks and soil. If it flows on the soil surface, it might wash past the urine and faeces left by animals, leaves that have fallen from trees, and decaying bodies of dead plants and animals. By the time it flows into a stream or pond the water may well have collected quite a lot of waste made by living creatures. But usually Nature sees to it that these impurities don't stay in the water very long.

Thousands of different kinds of microscopically small creatures live in the water and for many of them the waste made by other living things isn't dirt. It's food. Between them they can devour almost every kind of waste. As they do, they release their own waste chemicals into the water and this nourishes plants and other micro-organisms. And as the plants and smaller creatures grow and reproduce, they provide food for larger animals, including fish and other animals that serve as food for us.

Rivers carry impurities from the land that nourish the creatures of the sea and, working together, they can eventually remove or break down most impurities. Much of the waste is finally turned into water itself, or carbon dioxide which can escape from the water into the air.

Not all the impurities that water picks up can be used by living things, though. The ones that can't, collect in the sea. Some eventually sink to the ocean bottom or wash up on the shore. The rest of the impurities stay mixed with the water in the oceans and this is why seawater is salty. When the Earth's water first formed, the young oceans contained very little salt, but they have collected more and more salty impurities over thousands of millions of years.

...LARGER FISH! WHICH ARE EATEN BY PEOPLE!

Sunshine Disinfectant

For millions of years, the Earth's two main water cleaning systems have been at work recycling the Earth's water and providing a home and food for the things that live in water.

For animals that live on land, life is a little different. The water isn't their home, but they do need a regular supply of water to drink and this water has to be free of impurities that would make them ill. Micro-organisms in the water are especially a problem. Most of them are harmless and many are useful, but there are some which cause disease. Luckily there is another natural water cleaner that can make water safer for animals. It is the sun. Sunshine is a natural disinfectant.

The light from the sun contains ultraviolet (or UV) radiation. This is the radiation that gives us sunburn if we spend a long time in the sunshine without protecting our skin. Ultraviolet radiation can damage micro-organisms in the same way as it damages our skin, but for them, the damage is usually fatal.

Sunlight doesn't completely sterilize the water in rivers and lakes. If it did, all the useful cleaning micro-organisms would be killed as well as any harmful ones.

Ultraviolet rays can shine through water, but not very well. The radiation is only bright and powerful enough to damage micro-organisms on the surface. Those living a few centimetres below usually escape from harm.

But the disinfectant action of sunlight on the top layers of water is often enough to make water safe for animals to drink since they drink from the surface of lakes and rivers, not the bottom.

HIDE, HIDE, THE SUN'S OUT! THE SUN'S OUT!

Underground Storage and Cleaning

Every living thing needs water to survive. The problem with relying on rainfall to supply water is that it isn't very reliable. Many areas of the world get little rain and in some, all the rain falls in one season. Places like Britain get quite a lot of rainfall, but even so there can be long spells of dry weather when the animals and plants, which are used to having plenty of water, begin to suffer.

In most areas, there is a supply of water beneath the surface of the land that can last through the longest dry spell – groundwater. Remember that a lot of rainwater seeps into the soil when it falls. Underground, the water doesn't evaporate like water on the land surface. Some of it sinks through the soil into the earth. Water can even seep through some kinds of rock until it comes to a layer of waterproof rock which prevents it sinking deeper. In some places, water becomes trapped underground, but usually groundwater finds a channel which allows it to flow slowly down towards the sea.

Of course, if this water remained underground until it reached the sea, it would be of no use to the animals living on top of the ground, but groundwater comes to the surface in hollows and valleys where the level of the ground is below the level of the groundwater. Groundwater can also flow out of springs on a hillside to form the beginning of streams. The bottom of lakes is usually below the level of the groundwater and that is why most lakes still contain some water even during the longest dry spell.

You may think that water which has been in the dark, seeping through earth and rock, would contain a large number of micro-organisms and other impurities that might make it unsafe for animals to drink. Actually, the opposite is true. The earth and rock act as a very fine filter trapping micro-organisms and impurities to make the water cleaner tasting and safer to drink. So, as well as storing water, the ground can actually clean it.

The Beginning of Water Pollution

Many people believe that water pollution is a problem which only began a couple of hundred years ago when we started making new chemicals and releasing them into the environment. In fact, the problem is thousands of years old.

Human beings have been living on Earth for about 2½ million years, but until about 12,000 years ago our ancestors lived in pretty much the same way as many animals do. They had no permanent homes because they had to be on the move all the time searching for food. They collected rainwater when they could, and if it didn't rain they had to find a source of clean safe water wherever they travelled. Their waste was washed into the water and handled by the natural water cleaning systems.

They may have been living 'as Nature intended' but life could not have been easy. During hot dry weather, they had to stay near a river, lake or spring even if it meant going short of food. If the water there began to dry up, taste dirty or make them sick, they set off for another source of water, hoping it would be better. Many must have died on the way. The world's human population was very small – probably little more than 10 million.

Human life began to change about 12,000 years ago when people started settling down to get their food by growing crops and raising animals. This meant that for the first time in the history of the Earth, a large amount of faeces and urine began to collect in one place. And the easiest way to get rid of this waste was to make it wash away with nearby rivers and streams. As the settlements grew into villages, towns and then cities, the water around them became dirtier and dirtier.

People in towns liked to have homes beside the river or on bridges so they could have a 'privy' that jutted out over the water. This meant that their waste would drop down into the river and be washed away. Most people couldn't afford their own privy but public privies were often built over a flowing stream. Sometimes a large pit was dug and privies were built on top, but these were less convenient because they had to be emptied every so often.

Not everyone lived near to a public privy and many of those who did probably found using them a bit of a bother, especially at night. Many used chamber pots instead and would sometimes empty them onto the street. A great deal of dung was deposited in the street from horses, donkeys and other animals that used the roads so it's not surprising that people thought their own faeces could be dumped there as well. All this made crossing the street a very unpleasant experience. Sometimes people wore special wooden platform shoes so they could cross the street without getting their feet dirty. Some towns had foot bridges or stepping stones built across their streets.

When rainwater washed through a human settlement, it didn't just wash a little bit of waste into the nearby stream, lake or river, the water was flooded with waste.

Water full of human waste, or 'sewage' as we call it today, was the first water pollution problem and it is still one of the most serious water pollution problems that we face.

Why Sewage Harms the Environment

When large amounts of sewage are first washed into a river, lake or stream, the waste-eating bacteria living in the water have a feast. As they digest our waste, they release their own waste into the water, providing nutrients for plants and other living things. The population of smaller creatures, like bacteria and algae which can reproduce quickly, increases to take best advantage of the extra nourishment.

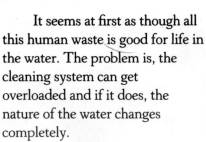

It seems at first as though all this human waste is good for life in the water. The problem is, the cleaning system can get overloaded and if it does, the nature of the water changes completely.

To work efficiently, the natural water cleaning system needs plenty of oxygen. Most water does contain oxygen because oxygen in the air easily mixes with water. But as they eat, grow and multiply, waste-eating micro-organisms use oxygen very quickly. If there are too many of them, they use up the oxygen more quickly than it can be replaced. Without sufficient oxygen, the waste-eating micro-organisms work more slowly and the fish and other water animals which need oxygen either swim away or slowly suffocate.

Meanwhile, the plants in the water can grow rapidly using the nutrients released from the sewage. The water becomes thick with algae and weeds. They eventually die and add to the waste in the water.

When oxygen gets very short, new micro-organisms that don't need oxygen begin to take over. These can also eat waste from the sewage and produce wastes of their own, but their wastes don't nourish the other living things in the water. In fact, they are poisonous to many creatures, including people.

Humans have been suffering the consequences of water pollution for thousands of years. In most cases, the sewage would not have completely destroyed life in the water, but people living in towns must have noticed the damage. It made fish scarce and the water smelly.

Something else worried them much more, however. Sewage is not just harmful to the things that live in the water. It is very harmful to us. And while it takes quite a lot of sewage to disrupt the life of a river, it takes only a little to disrupt and even end our own lives.

I'M FEEDING MY MICRO-ORGANISMS!

Why Sewage Makes Us Sick

We don't need to be taught that drinking water contaminated with sewage is bad for us. It is so important for us to know this that we know it instinctively. The very idea of it makes us feel sick. But what exactly is so harmful about the waste from human bodies?

It's the faeces that are the main danger. They are full of undigested food and bacteria. The undigested food is there because most food we eat contains some substances we simply *can't* digest. We can't, for example, digest bran. The bacteria are there because they *can* get goodness from bran and many of the other indigestible substances we swallow. Billions of bacteria live at the end part of the digestive system where they feast on the leftovers from our meals.

Many other animals also have bacteria living in their digestive systems and it is perfectly normal and healthy for bacteria to be there. Very often the bacteria provide the animal with substances vital to its survival. The bacteria living in our digestive systems, for example, make vitamin K and perhaps many other necessary substances.

THIS ONE LOOKS LIKE TROUBLE

The problem is that the digestive system can also provide a home for micro-organisms that are not so helpful – bacteria, viruses and other microscopically small creatures which cause disease. Again, humans aren't the only animals that have disease-causing microbes in their faeces. But our sewage is particularly dangerous to us because the kinds of micro-organisms it contains have already infected people, so they are the kinds most likely to infect other people.

Very often these micro-organisms do their damage by disrupting the digestive system, causing vomiting, diarrhoea or both. Not only is this painful and unpleasant, it can be fatal. It causes a loss of body fluid and, in serious cases, victims lose so much of this fluid, the body can no longer work properly.

In the past, bacteria which cause serious diseases like cholera have got into the water supply of a city or town and killed thousands of people. The last major cholera outbreaks in Britain were in the first part of the nineteenth century. Many people in London, Bristol, Exeter and several other cities died of the disease.

Not all the micro-organisms that can contaminate sewage are as deadly as the bacteria which causes cholera. Vomiting and diarrhoea are often the body's ways of getting rid of harmful micro-organisms. It flushes them out of the digestive system. But that only means that the problem has been flushed away with the sewage. If that sewage contaminates the water other people drink, they will catch the infection.

It's possible to become immune to some of the micro-organisms which infect our digestive system. They usually cause sickness for a short time and then, once we become immune, they quietly take up permanent residence in our digestive system. They grow and multiply there so that afterwards our faeces always contain a few million of these micro-organisms ready to cause illness if they get a chance to infect someone who isn't immune.

Some people find they fall ill when they go abroad on holiday and drink or swim in the local water. The people who live in the area often refuse to believe there is anything wrong with their water because it never does *them* any harm. This may be because they already have the local disease-causing bacteria or viruses living inside their digestive systems and are immune to them.

It is not only the digestive system that is attacked by the micro-organisms from human waste. The crippling disease called polio is often caught by drinking or swimming in water containing sewage. The virus that causes polio enters the body through the digestive system but then attacks and damages the nerves in the spine.

Many children in Britain used to catch polio and some of the people in wheelchairs today were crippled by it when they were younger. Nowadays, though, there is a vaccine which can protect people from polio. Do you remember being given a drop of polio vaccine on a sugar cube? It contains a harmless relative of the polio virus that takes up residence inside your digestive system making you immune to the virus that does the damage.

No one would choose to drink water that is contaminated with sewage but what can you do to prevent it? Our ancestors began to find answers to this question many years ago.

Clean Water Science Begins

Less than 150 years ago people found out that micro-organisms cause disease. Three hundred and fifty years ago they didn't even know micro-organisms existed. In those days people had no way of telling for sure whether or not the water they were going to drink would make them ill. But once water pollution became a problem, it didn't take our ancestors long to find ways of dealing with it. The first discoveries in the science of clean water were made thousands of years ago.

The best way to deal with water pollution is to prevent it. In many towns, human and animal waste was regularly collected and carted out into the countryside. This not only prevented it being dumped in the water, it also provided nearby farmers with excellent fertilizer. Bacteria in soil can feed on the waste and release its nutrients in the same way as the water bacteria do. Our ancestors found that digging faeces into soil made their crops more successful.

In spite of this, the water in lakes, rivers and streams near to human settlements was often not safe to drink. No one knows who first discovered that polluted water could be made safer by boiling it for a few minutes, but it has been done for thousands of years and it works. Boiling the dirty water didn't improve its taste, though, and people may have first begun drinking tea to cover up the taste of the water. This may also have been why people started to believe that tea is 'healthy' or 'medicinal'. It often was healthier to drink tea but this was usually because boiling the water had killed the micro-organisms it contained.

The problem with boiling as a method of cleaning water is that it takes fuel, and many of our ancestors couldn't afford to buy enough fuel to boil all their water as well as do their cooking. It was more economical to look for

sources of clean water. And our ancestors became very good at finding them.

Many had containers for collecting and saving rainwater. If this ran out they had to collect more from a safe source. In some places, only the water downstream of the town or village was polluted, so people collected safe water by going upstream. (This was probably why, in the nursery rhyme, Jack and Jill went *up* the hill to fetch a pail of water.)

One of the most important discoveries our ancestors made was groundwater. People had known for thousands, perhaps millions, of years that water which wells up from the ground in springs is usually safe to drink. But then someone realized that water in the springs had to come from somewhere and that there was probably a supply of safe water underground. They began digging holes or 'wells' to get at this water, and once they had dug deep enough to get below the level of the groundwater, they found it. No one knows when the first wells were dug but archaeologists have found towns built in India more than 4,500 years ago with a very sophisticated systems of wells.

I THINK IT'S JUST DAMP!

Once towns grew into cities and people became better builders, they found they could collect and store rainwater on a very large scale. They built dams across rivers and streams to trap and store the water. This created artificial lakes or 'reservoirs' which were often large enough to supply a whole town with water through a long dry spell. In some towns they even dug artificial rivers or tunnels for the water to flow along so it would reach the areas where it was needed.

The ancient water scientists didn't know about ultraviolet radiation in sunshine and had no idea that it killed micro-organisms in the water, but they might have noticed that water became safer while it was stored in the reservoir. Some worked out that they could make it cleaner if they filtered the water through a layer of sand, trapping bits of dirt and some bacteria. The thicker the layer of sand, the cleaner the water would be.

Many of the methods of getting clean water which were developed in ancient times are still used today. There's a good chance that the water flowing out of your taps comes either from a well or a reservoir and it was probably filtered through a bed of sand.

Making Tap Water

When you think how hard some of our ancestors had to work to get safe drinking water, it seems incredible that nowadays we can have a bath, wash the car, water the garden and even put out fires with water that is clean enough to drink. This change wasn't brought about by one huge scientific breakthrough. A whole series of scientific and technical breakthroughs was needed before it became possible to build the system that brings us tap water.

Complicated building work is often needed to dam and re-route rivers. Durable underground pipes and powerful pumps have to be installed to move massive amounts of water long distances. Sometimes wells must be drilled hundreds of metres deep to reach underground water. Tests must be performed to find out what impurities the water contains, and those which are harmful or troublesome have to be removed. And finally, a complex network of pipes is needed to deliver the water to every home, office and factory.

A number of natural sources of water have been found that are perfectly safe to drink. But these are usually in remote country locations far away from the cities

where most people live. Naturally clean water is usually groundwater and, if it has picked up substances – minerals from the rocks underground which give it a nice taste, it is often bottled and sold as 'mineral water'. Some people prefer to drink mineral water but not many people could afford to have a shower in it.

Most water in Nature contains impurities that might cause illness but that isn't the only problem. Some natural water contains mineral impurities in such large concentrations there is a danger they will block pipes or cause metals to rust. And there are some quite harmless impurities that simply make the water unpleasant. They give it a funny taste, smell or appearance.

The impurities are dealt with at a water treatment works. The largest treatment works receive more than 200,000 litres of water every minute. It flows out again about 8 hours later as tap water with many of its impurities taken away and a few new ones added.

ONE GLASS OF WATER COMING DOWN!

TEA 45p
(FFEE 50
SONE 30
CHIPS 70
COKE 60
WATER £3..

PLEASE PAY HERE

Over the years, chemists have developed many different ways of removing impurities but no single method can deal with all the troublesome impurities water contains. Most water treatment works use a number of different methods.

Think for a minute about how you might go about removing impurities from water. Imagine someone giving you a pot of cold tea and asking you to remove enough of the impurities to make it look, taste and smell like water. How would you do it? It's difficult because the chemicals that give tea its taste and colour aren't just floating around in the water. They have 'dissolved'. They have become so thoroughly mixed with the water, they are almost part of it.

The old method of filtering the water through a bed of sand is still used at many works. In most cases, the water is made to flow quite rapidly through a bed of sand about a metre thick. This removes larger particles but allows small particles and dissolved chemicals to flow right through. Chemists have developed other substances that can attract and stick to bacteria, viruses and even certain chemicals that have dissolved in the water.

They have also found that certain chemicals will react with some of water's troublesome impurities and change them so they can no longer mix with water. Adding a carefully calculated mix of chemicals makes the impurities collect together in wispy strands called 'flocs'. The flocs gently sink to the bottom of 'settling tanks' and much clearer better-tasting water flows from the top of the tank.

To get an idea of how this works, why not try this experiment with milk and vinegar. Milk is mostly water although it contains a large number of different impurities. Pour a few drops of vinegar into a glass of milk, gently stirring the milk to mix the chemicals. Keep adding vinegar until you see a change in the milk. Vinegar is much more acidic than the milk and this makes it impossible for many of the substances in milk to stay mixed with the water.

37

Some other water treatment methods don't remove troublesome impurities at all. They just change them into less troublesome impurities. For example, a harmless brown chemical in the water is only troublesome because it makes the water look brown. Changing it into a colourless chemical is often enough to solve the problem. Impurities that give the water a funny taste or smell can often be dealt with in the same way.

The sorts of methods which are used at a water treatment works depend on what the water is like when it enters the works. The sorts and amounts of impurities that water contains can be very different in different areas.

Many of the treatments used succeed in removing bacteria and viruses and other micro-organisms from the water, but even a small number of micro-organisms could cause an outbreak of serious illness. To be absolutely sure the water is safe to drink, the water is disinfected before it leaves the treatment works.,

Remember how ultraviolet radiation in sunshine kills micro-organisms? Some water treatment works copy this natural method of disinfection and make the water flow through a beam of ultraviolet radiation shining from special electric lights.

It is more common though to

PRICES
LADIES £7.00
GENTS £5.00
CHILD £3.50
TROUBLESOME
IMPURITIES...
£25.00

add a chemical such as chlorine to the water to disinfect it. A small amount of chlorine can kill bacteria and viruses but it doesn't make the water unsafe for humans to drink. As this 'chlorinated' water travels along the pipes to your home, the chlorine gradually leaves the water and enters the air, but some of it is still there when it arrives at your tap. The advantage of this is that the chlorine is still there disinfecting the water. The disadvantage is that chlorine gives the water a taste that some people don't like.

Even though they have become experts at cleaning water, the chemists and engineers that design treatment works rely as much as possible on Nature's ability to clean water. They try to make sure the water that enters the treatment works is as clean as Nature can make it. When the natural water contains high concentrations of troublesome impurities, more treatments or more expensive treatments have to be used and the quality of the tap water is often not as good.

In some parts of the world, where very little fresh water is naturally available, a supply of water is sometimes obtained by treating seawater to remove salt. Large 'desalination' plants usually heat the seawater to make it evaporate and then allow the fresh water to condense (see Chapter 3). Another method is to freeze the seawater. This works because the water separates from the salt when it forms into ice crystals. If you put seawater in a freezer and collect any ice that forms, you will find that it has lost a lot of its salty taste.

Why not contact the company or authority responsible for supplying your water? They will be able to tell you where your tap water comes from and what sorts of treatment it has received before it reaches your home. They might even let you or your class pay a visit to a water treatment works.

CHLORINE!

Treating Sewage

A great deal of work goes into making water clean and piping it to the taps in your home. Then you dirty it and send it away down more pipes. It must then be cleaned again so that it can flow harmlessly into rivers, lakes or the sea.

Treatment of this dirty water is very different from the treatment the water had before it arrived at your home. Chemists can claim a lot of the credit for the methods that turn natural water into your tap water. The job of turning your sewage back into natural water is done almost entirely by Nature.

In most modern towns and cities, waste water is piped to a sewage treatment works to be cleaned. In the country, waste water is often treated in a septic tank.

A septic tank is usually nothing more than a small underground room with a pipe to bring in dirty water, another pipe to let cleaner water trickle out, and a sort of chimney in the roof. It seems incredible that such a simple structure can do the important and complicated job of cleaning sewage.

It works because a septic tank provides an ideal home for billions of waste-eating micro-organisms. They are the micro-organisms which would naturally inhabit a very polluted pond which contains very little oxygen (see page 25). As dirty water flows into a septic tank, the worst of the dirt begins to settle. Micro-organisms searching for food cling to pieces of dirt and cause them to sink down into a layer of 'sludge' at the bottom of the tank, leaving a layer of quite clean water near the top.

This water trickles out of the tank and flows over an area of stones or tiles. The water can pick up a lot of oxygen from the air as it flows and the stones or tiles soon become covered in a slime which contains billions more micro-organisms. Using the oxygen in the water, they can very quickly digest most of the rest of dirt, leaving the water clean enough to flow harmlessly into a stream.

Meanwhile, the dirt that remained inside the tank is much more slowly digested by bacteria that don't need oxygen. There are hundreds of different kinds of bacteria and between them they can eat grease, soap, detergent, toilet paper, the undigested food, bacteria and chemicals that make up our faeces and urine and most other things that come their way. They can't digest plastic and are harmed by some chemicals, so people who use septic tanks have to be a bit careful what they put down the drain.

BURP

Like all living creatures, the bacteria inside septic tanks make waste of their own. This is often in the form of gases that bubble to the surface of the water and escape through the hole in the roof. As well as bacteria, septic tank sludge contains creatures that eat bacteria and they, in turn, are eaten by larger predators. Every septic tank is a complex natural community with more inhabitants than the entire human population of the Earth. The creatures are so good at eating up dirt and each other that most septic tanks only need some of their sludge emptying every few years. It is usually taken by tanker lorry to the nearest sewage treatment works.

It would be impossible to use septic tanks to treat the sewage from a large town or city. Each tank needs quite a lot of space to handle a small amount of waste. Sewage treatment works are needed to handle dirty water on a large scale. These works also rely on billions and billions of micro-organisms to do most of the work of cleaning the water, and they are designed to encourage the micro-organisms to work quickly and in a small space. They are often called 'sewage farms' and they really are like farms except that the plants and animals they raise are microscopically small.

43

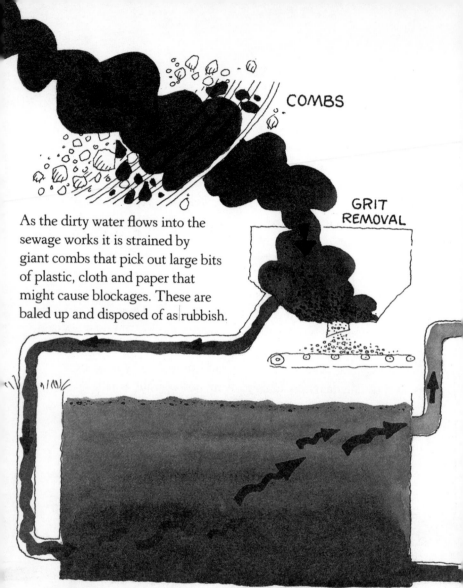

COMBS

GRIT
REMOVAL

As the dirty water flows into the sewage works it is strained by giant combs that pick out large bits of plastic, cloth and paper that might cause blockages. These are baled up and disposed of as rubbish.

SETTLEMENT TANK

The flow of the water is then slowed down as it is piped into large calm ponds called 'settlement tanks' where pieces of dirt float to the top or sink to the bottom of the water. The water containing most of the dirt (called sludge) is removed and piped to 'sludge digesters' to be worked on by micro-organisms which don't need oxygen. The cleanest water flows on to be treated by fast-acting micro-organisms which do use oxygen, either with 'activated sludge' or in 'trickle tanks'.

Activated sludge is a mixture of waste-eating micro-organisms. This mix is added to the water and compressed air is bubbled very quickly through the water. The more dirt the water contains, the longer the activated sludge needs to work on it, but at most sewage works, the process only takes about 8 hours.

AERATION TANK

FINAL SETTLEMENT TANK

After that, the water is allowed to stand for a while in 'final settlement tanks'. Clean water flows out over the top of the tanks while the activated sludge organisms settle to the bottom.

Some of this sludge is piped out and mixed with more dirty water in need of treatment. But because the micro-organisms grow and reproduce while they work, extra activated sludge is created with each treatment. This is piped to the sludge digesters.

In other sewage works the micro-organisms do their cleaning in 'trickle tanks'. These contain a bed of stones about two metres deep. The stones are round or oval and about 20 centimetres in diameter. Each one is covered with a slime that is full of waste-eating micro-organisms. Dirty water is sprinkled onto the stones from arms that travel over the bed of stones and, as it trickles down over the slime, the micro-organisms remove and digest the dirt.

Water treated in a trickle tank or by activated sludge no longer contains many disease-causing micro-organisms and is clean enough to be released into most bodies of water without harming the natural life. But if tests show that this life is in danger, the sewage will need added treatments such as those used to clean tap water (see Chapter 11).

GAS

SLUDGE DIGESTER

Meanwhile, back at the sewage farm, the very dirty water is still being treated by micro-organisms in the sludge digesters. They spend a few weeks breaking down the large, complicated and sometimes smelly chemicals that the waste contains. They kill and digest the micro-organisms in the waste, including the ones which cause disease. And as they work, the micro-organisms release gases which can be burned to produce heat or electricity. Some sewage works save a great deal of money by generating their own electricity with the gas from their sludge digesters.

The micro-organisms in the sludge digesters can't turn all the waste into burnable gas. Their leftovers collect at the bottom of the digester as 'digested sludge'.

If the sewage works has had to treat waste water from factories, the digested sludge may contain some poisonous metals like lead or cadmium which the micro-organisms can't break down. If not, it can be used as a fertilizer on farms or mixed with other forms of waste and made into garden compost. However, a lot of digested sludge is simply disposed of like rubbish or dumped at sea for the waste-eating creatures there to handle.

Many people believe that it is wrong to tip sewage sludge into the sea, especially if it contains poisonous metals, because it could damage the natural life in the seawater. Others are also concerned that sewage sludge is being wasted while other natural resources are being used to make fertilizer and compost.

But deciding on the best ways of dealing with sewage sludge is only one of the problems that the science of cleaning water has to solve.

Clean Water Costs Money

We now know how to solve the water pollution problems that our ancestors had to live with for thousands of years. We know how to make sure water is safe to drink. We know how to treat sewage so that it doesn't harm the natural life in lakes, rivers or the sea. So why are the water pollution problems on Earth greater than they have ever been?

There are, of course, more people on Earth, and our waste water contains a more complex mix of chemicals. But the main problem is that clean water costs money. Systems to supply clean water and dispose of sewage have to be built, kept running and kept in good repair. In Britain and many other countries, everyone who uses the water systems is expected to pay towards the cost. It is, perhaps, human nature that most people want to pay as little as possible.

Everyone can see the value of investing in a system to bring them safe drinking water but it is not so obvious that cleaning waste water is equally important. However, many people have now discovered the problems that arise if waste water is not treated well enough to prevent it damaging the natural life in lakes, rivers and seas.

Many years ago, some authorities believed the most

economical way to deal with untreated sewage was to pump it into the sea for the waste-eating micro-organisms there to digest. But they found that without careful planning, much of it washed back towards the shore, bringing bits of plastic, cloth, paper and other floating debris as well as dangerous bacteria and viruses.

Bodies of water which have already been polluted will not recover until improvements are made to the treatment of waste water from the surrounding area. This will cost money. But it's not just the living things in the water that suffer from pollution. We do as well.

If the life in the water is damaged, so are the natural water cleaning systems, and that can affect the quality of our drinking water. In some areas, people complain that the tap water may be safe to drink but it simply doesn't taste nice. Often the problem is the natural water. If the water treatment works are forced to take in natural water which contains a large number of some impurities, the treated water won't taste so nice. More expensive treatments can improve the taste of water, but it might be better to spend the money on sewage treatment to improve the quality of the natural water. Either way, it costs money.

But these are the money problems of the wealthier people in the world. For most people on Earth, the problem is much more desperate. Lack of money means that they still have to suffer the problems of dirty water which science and technology have conquered for us. Many people have to travel long distances to collect safe water to drink. And in many areas, there is often no safe drinking water at all.

The deadly disease cholera is still a danger. There were outbreaks of cholera in some of the Ethiopian refugee camps during the famines in the late 1980s. Polio still cripples and kills children in countries where people can afford neither clean water nor the protective vaccine. And people who are weak and poorly nourished are victims of many of the other micro-organisms dirty water can contain.

The World Health Organization has estimated that over 80 per cent of the disease in the world today is caused by contaminated water. In poor countries, infections carried in the water supply kill over 30,000 children every day.

A great deal of suffering could be prevented by small local projects to dig wells, protect springs from contamination, build privies or lay a pipe to bring water to a village. The projects don't cost much individually, but so many people need help that a great deal of money is needed. Many international aid charities such as Save the Children and Oxfam believe providing safe water is among the most important things they are doing to help the people in developing countries.

When we are deciding how much money to spend on cleaning water in our own country, we should not forget the problems of people in other countries. If you would like to learn more and help raise money, you will find addresses on page 62 of some charities such as Water Aid which are funding safe water projects.

51

New Pollution Problems

Modern technology, if you can afford it, makes it possible to solve the old problems of sewage pollution and contaminated drinking water. But our modern way of life has also made the problem of water pollution much more complicated.

In the last 200 years, a vast range of new technologies have been developed that are making the lives of people in the wealthier countries easier and more interesting than ever before. We don't just have plenty of safe drinking water. Modern methods of farming have made food plentiful. Coal, oil, gas and electricity keep us warm and provide energy for the machines that do much of our work. Modern factories produce a whole range of new things for us to use, wear, look at, listen to or play with.

The problem is, almost all of these new technologies have had an effect on the natural environment in some way. So many of the manufactured

NOW I KNOW WHAT THEY MEAN ABOUT THE EFFLUENT SOCIETY!

products that we take for granted – from televisions to knives and forks . . . from the clothes we wear to the coat of paint on the walls – cannot be made without the use of substances which can be very damaging to the environment. Many of them have been accidentally or intentionally released into the Earth's waters. The creatures living there have had to cope with many impurities they have never encountered before.

In the past, some factories poured large amounts of waste water into nearby rivers or the sea without pausing to think about the lethal chemicals it contained. Nowadays manufacturers must be more responsible, and better treatments to remove poisonous impurities from waste water are planned for the future. These treatments will be expensive, however. We will have to be prepared to pay more for products made in clean factories.

Preventing modern pollution problems requires more than just money, however. It is also essential to get the science right. Scientists now understand far better why some chemicals damage the environment and how this damage can be avoided.

Is It Biodegradable?

Many people regularly pour chemicals such as bleach into the toilet to 'kill germs'. These disinfectants are usually very poisonous substances specially chosen for their ability to destroy bacteria and it may seem as though flushing them down the toilet would be a disaster for the useful bacteria in the water and at the sewage farm. It isn't. The most powerful household disinfectants lose their power once they are diluted by the rest of the water in the drain. They often react with sunlight and other substances in the water and turn into less harmful substances. Some disinfectants can actually serve as food for micro-organisms at the sewage farm.

Scientists now know that it's important to find out whether or not a new chemical is 'biodegradable' – whether or not it will be quickly broken down in the environment. If Nature can't destroy them, washing poisonous substances away is not the answer because they just build up in the sea. And even relatively harmless chemicals can become a problem if they can't be destroyed.

THEY'RE ONLY DANGEROUS WHEN THEY'RE ALL TOGETHER!

Have you seen 'biodegradable' written on a packet of detergent? In the 1940s and 50s chemists invented new detergents for washing clothes and dishes. The new detergents seemed to be no more harmful than the soap that people had been using for centuries but the chemists didn't realize that, while soap is easily broken down by waste-eating micro-organisms in the water, their new detergents were almost indigestible. They flowed out of people's washing machines and began to build up in streams and rivers. Some bodies of water even had suds floating on top.

The chemists quickly began to invent more new detergents, and this time made sure that they could be broken down by micro-organisms. Several years ago, Britain and most other countries passed a law that only these sorts of detergents can be sold for use in the home. So the detergent your family uses is biodegradable, even if it doesn't say so on the packet.

Detergents were never meant to harm living things in the environment but chemists have also invented a large range of chemicals to do just that – to kill creatures that attack crops and damage the health of farm animals. This is one of the reasons we have such plentiful supplies of food. But while there may be benefits to killing weeds, insects, mould, slugs, bacteria and parasites on the farm, we don't want these chemicals to keep on killing as they wash into the nearby streams, lakes and rivers.

Today, these new chemicals are tested to see how easily they will wash into the water, how quickly they are broken down and how much damage they might do before they are broken down. But there are still problems. Will tests be effective? Can they really tell us whether or not a chemical could harm each of the vast number of living things it might meet as it flows along in the water? The problems of the past still haunt us, too. Many older chemicals haven't been environmentally tested and probably wouldn't pass today's tests. Yet some of them are still being used and still being released into the environment.

Making sure substances are biodegradable is by no means the answer to all our new pollution problems. Some substances cause pollution because they provide living things with too much nourishment and cause problems similar to those caused by sewage pollution.

Nitrogen and phosphorus are nutrients which plants need to grow, but if large amounts of chemicals containing these elements are allowed to get in the water, plants such as algae can grow so quickly that they upset the natural balance of living things in the water.

All human and animal waste contains a great deal of phosphorus but the waste water from our homes today contains even more because a compound containing phosphorus is in most of the powders and liquids we use to wash our clothes. Farming adds to the levels of both phosphorus and nitrogen in the water. Fertilizing farmland, whether it is with powdered fertilizers, manure or compost, increases the risk of water becoming overloaded with phosphorus and nitrogen. But again, our plentiful supplies of food depend on farmers using fertilizer.

Energy and Water Pollution

Our modern way of life is only possible because of the vast amount of energy we use. Getting the energy we need has meant oil and radioactive elements being accidentally and sometimes intentionally released into the water. And the air pollution caused by the burning of coal and oil has caused water to be polluted before it even rains to the ground.

In the first half of the twentieth century, the skies over some areas of Britain were thick with smoke from coal fires. The water in the rain, mist and fog was sometimes more acidic than vinegar. People suffered lung problems from breathing in this fog and the stone of many buildings and statues was dissolved away by the acid. You may have noticed the damage caused by acid rain if you have looked at old stone carvings.

This is because burning these fuels can release chemicals into the air that mix with the droplets of water in the clouds. Two of these chemicals, sulphur dioxide and nitrogen dioxide, combine with water to become sulphuric and nitric acid. The rain falling from these polluted clouds is acid rain.

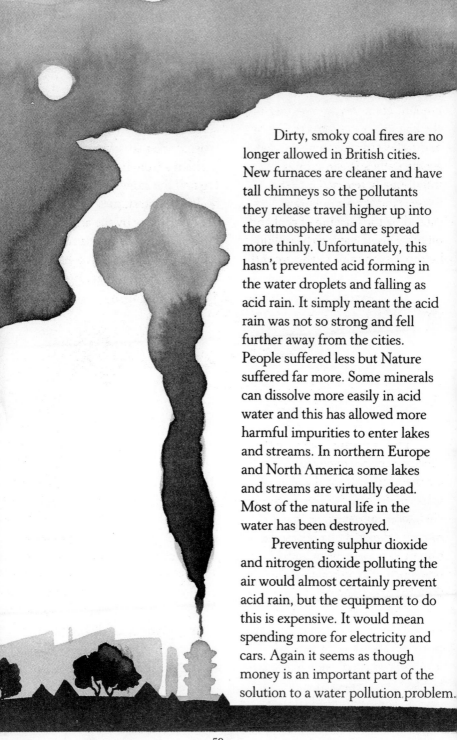

Dirty, smoky coal fires are no longer allowed in British cities. New furnaces are cleaner and have tall chimneys so the pollutants they release travel higher up into the atmosphere and are spread more thinly. Unfortunately, this hasn't prevented acid forming in the water droplets and falling as acid rain. It simply meant the acid rain was not so strong and fell further away from the cities. People suffered less but Nature suffered far more. Some minerals can dissolve more easily in acid water and this has allowed more harmful impurities to enter lakes and streams. In northern Europe and North America some lakes and streams are virtually dead. Most of the natural life in the water has been destroyed.

Preventing sulphur dioxide and nitrogen dioxide polluting the air would almost certainly prevent acid rain, but the equipment to do this is expensive. It would mean spending more for electricity and cars. Again it seems as though money is an important part of the solution to a water pollution problem.

But burning coal, oil and gas may be helping to bring on a far more serious threat which will affect the basic natural system that all land animals rely on to provide clean water.

Burning causes the gas, carbon dioxide, to be released into the air. It is normal for air to contain a little carbon dioxide, but over the last 200 years, people have burned a great deal of coal, oil and gas to get the energy they need, and this has caused the levels of carbon dioxide in the air to rise. The extra carbon dioxide isn't poisoning anything, but it,

along with some other gases that people have allowed to pollute the air, seems to be causing the whole world to become slightly warmer.

This is what scientists call the 'greenhouse effect'. They aren't sure what the results of this 'global warming' will be, but many fear that it could change the Earth's weather patterns. This could be devastating. Areas that now have plenty of rainfall could become much drier, causing crops to fail and people to starve. Other areas could get more rain and suffer destructive flooding.

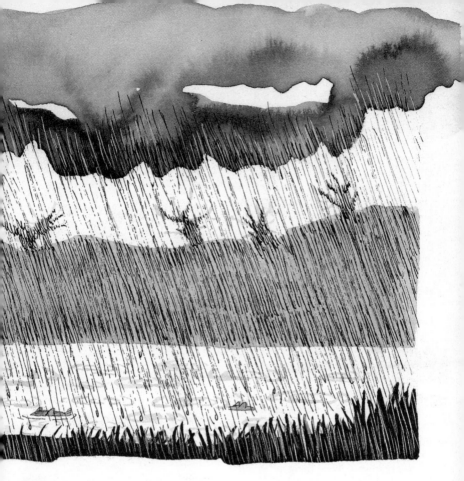

What Can Be Done?

The kinds of lives we lead today depend on modern technology, but our lives depend even more on the Earth's natural systems which provide us with resources as vital as clean water. Very few of us would like to go back to the sort of life people led 200 years ago when sewage was the only water pollution problem. But if we have to pay more for things in order to ensure they don't harm the environment we might not be able to afford some of the benefits of modern technology.

The problems can't be solved by individuals or even individual countries. One thing is for certain, we cannot abandon modern technology. We have to find a balance that allows modern life to exist beside a healthy environment. And we have to help the poorer people of the world gain some of the benefits technology has brought to us in the richer countries.

Glossary

acid rain rain polluted with sulphuric or nitric acid

algae minute water plants

bacteria the smallest and simplest living creatures

biodegradable capable of being broken down in the natural environment

chlorine chemical used to disinfect water

condensation changing from a gas to a liquid or solid

disinfectant a substance which kills bacteria

dissolve mix with a liquid to become evenly spread through the liquid

evaporation changing from a liquid or solid to a gas

faeces human waste

filter device for removing particles from liquids

global warming gradual increase in the temperature of the Earth

immune not affected by

impurity a substance that has mixed with another substance so that it is no longer pure

microbes minute living things

micro-organisms living thing not visible to the naked eye

mineral water groundwater that has picked up mineral impurities from the rocks and soil

nitrogen a substance which can be a gas and form part of the air but which can also join with other chemicals to become part of living things

nutrient food or other substance essential to living things

phosphorus a substance which living things need to live and grow

polio infectious disease which damages the nerves in the spine

privy lavatory without a water supply for taking away the waste

recycle convert waste to reusable material

septic tank underground container in which sewage is treated

ultraviolet radiation radiation similar to light which cannot be detected by the human eye

vapour gaseous form of normally liquid substance

virus tiny particle which infects living things

Useful Addresses

In Britain:

CAFOD
2 Romero Close, London SW9 9TY

Centre for World Development
Information
Regent's College, Regent's Park,
London NW1 4NS

Christian Aid
PO Box 100, London SE1 7RT

National Association of Development
Education Centres
6 Endsleigh Street, London WC1H 0DX

Oxfam
274 Banbury Road, Oxford OX2 7DZ

Save the Children
Mary Datelor House, 17 Grove Lane,
London SE5 8RD

UNICEF-UK
55 Lincoln's Inn Fields,
London WC2 3NB

Water Aid
1 Queen Anne's Gate,
London SW1H 9BT

In Eire:

Trocaire
169 Booterstown Avenue, Co. Dublin